Diana

© 1997 Grandreams Ltd

Written by Anthony Laurence
Designed by Jason Bazini
Photographs by All Action

Published by
Grandreams Limited
435-437 Edgware Road
Little Venice
London W2 1TH

Printed in Belgium

£4.99

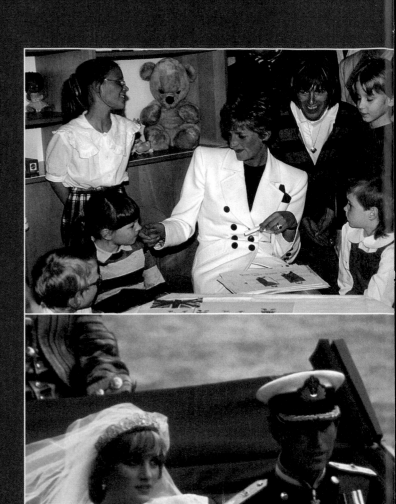

*D*iana, Princess of Wales, was without doubt the world's most famous woman. In terms of charm and charisma, few others came close to her.

The news that she had died so tragically in the early hours of 31 August 1997, came as a great shock to everyone in Great Britain and around the world.

In this tribute we, at Grandreams, look back at the fascinating story of 'the People's Princess' and the way she touched the lives of others wherever she went...

The Young *Diana*

A number of historical events occurred in 1961...

In January, 43-year-old John F. Kennedy was sworn in as the youngest ever President of the USA.

In April, the Soviet Union won the first leg of the Space Race by successfully launching a 27-year-old Army Major, Yuri Gagarin, into a 108-minute orbit around Earth aboard a Vostok spaceship. April also saw the USA and the Soviet Union almost on the brink of conflict over the 'Bay of Pigs' affair in Cuba.

In May, ex-British diplomat George Blake was jailed for spying for the Russians... and in sport, Tottenham Hotspur became the first team in the 20th century to secure the coveted League and FA Cup 'double'.

Later in the year, at an airport in France, the Russian ballet dancer Rudolf Nureyev defected to the west.

A British boxer, Terry Downes, won the middleweight championship of the world.

In East Germany, the notorious Berlin Wall was heightened and strengthened, thereby increasing the Cold War tension between east and west.

Future pop legends The Beatles and Bob Dylan were launching their respective careers... and at the cinema crowds were flocking to see the brilliant musical *West Side Story*.

In 1961, the British Royal Family was still basking in a warm glow of public affection following two happy events in the previous year. Princess Margaret had married the well-known photographer Antony Armstrong-Jones, and the Queen had given birth to her second son, Prince Andrew.

On 14 November 1961 Prince Charles, heir to the throne, enjoyed his thirteenth birthday.

Just four-and-a-half months earlier another, largely unnoticed, moment of history had taken place: namely the birth of The Honourable Diana Frances Spencer, the girl destined to become Prince Charles' wife and the future Princess of Wales.

The happy event occurred at Park House, on the royal estate at Sandringham, on 1 July 1961. The bouncing baby girl was the third daughter born to the then Viscount and Viscountess Althorp. Diana's elder sisters were Sarah (born in 1955) and Jane (born in 1957). A brother, Charles (the present Earl Spencer), would arrive three years later.

Diana's father, Edward John, had once been an equerry to King George VI and later Queen Elizabeth II.

Her mother, Frances Ruth, was the daughter of Lady Formoy, a lady-in-waiting to the Queen Mother.

Diana grew into a kind-hearted child with a fondness for cuddly toys and small furry animals. Among her playmates at Sandringham were the royal princes, Andrew and Edward – who often enjoyed a dip in the swimming pool at Park House.

In 1967, when Diana was six, she and her sisters and brother were devastated by the separation of their parents. Divorce followed and, after a long and acrimonious courtroom battle, the Viscount eventually won custody of the children. Diana's mother remarried in 1969, to Peter Shand-Kydd, and the children would often visit her at her new home in Sussex and later in Scotland.

The education of the young Diana Spencer was initially supervised by her governess, Gertrude Allen, in the schoolroom at Park House. Then, in 1968, she attended Silfield, a private day school in King's Lynn. She was a cheerful, popular pupil who loved reading and was complimented on her handwriting.

After two years the future Princess became a boarder at Riddlesworth Hall, a

Diana's father, the 8th Earl Spencer

Diana's mother, now Mrs Shand-Kydd

preparatory school for girls near Diss, within thirty miles of her home at Sandringham.

Again she was well-liked and was considered a very capable pupil. Although not particularly academic, she loved sports and games and was a very good swimmer. The caring side of her nature was also apparent and she was given charge of the school's prize-winning guinea pig known as 'Peanuts'.

At the age of twelve, Diana moved to her mother's old school, West Heath, an exclusive establishment for the daughters of well-heeled families, near Sevenoaks in Kent. She would remain as a boarding pupil until she was sixteen. During that time she continued to excel at sports and swimming and won several trophies. She enjoyed playing and watching tennis and when possible would accompany her mother to the first Saturday of the Wimbledon tennis championships.

Diana became a keen dancer during this period, and for a while wanted to become a ballerina. She literally grew out of that ambition, but would retain a great love of ballet for the rest of her life.

She also developed a compassionate interest in the care of handicapped children and the elderly. This led to a special award, presented to her in her last term at West Heath.

In 1975, Diana became Lady Diana Spencer when her father became the 8th Earl Spencer, following the death of her grandfather. This meant leaving Park House, the home she had always known.

The Earl and his family moved into Althorp House, a vast stately home in Northamptonshire built by Diana's ancestors over 500 years ago.

In the summer of 1976, Earl Spencer married again. His new bride was Raine, former

The Young Diana

Countess of Dartmouth and the daughter of the prolific romantic novelist Barbara Cartland.

One day in the winter of 1977, Althorp had a very special visitor – none other than the Prince of Wales himself, who was a guest of Diana's sister Sarah at a shooting party. At that time Sarah's name was linked romantically with the royal visitor.

Prince Charles had once said that 30 was the ideal age at which to marry. He was now 29, and was providing the newspapers with much copy in their constant quest for the answer to the question: *Who Will Marry the Future King?*

No-one realised it at the time, but the answer began to formulate when the 16-year-old Diana met the Prince in the middle of a ploughed field on the Althorp estate. She thought him to be 'pretty amazing', and he later described her as '...jolly and amusing and attractive...'

A few weeks later, Diana went off to a finishing school, the Institut Alpin Videmanette, at Gstaadt in Switzerland. She intended to stay for three months, but was soon suffering pangs of homesickness and returned to England after just six weeks.

By now, Diana was living in London – first at her mother's house in Cadogan Place,

Chelsea, later at a flat of her own, which she shared with three girlfriends, in Coleherne Court, South Kensington.

Lady Diana had decided that her future career would involve children. Her working life started as a nanny to an American child (whose parents she later invited to her wedding). For a while she was a student teacher in a Kensington dance studio where she kept a watchful eye over the young pupils. Then she became an assistant teacher at The Young England Kindergarten in St George's Square, Pimlico.

Diana's romance with the Prince of Wales began to blossom in private in 1980, after the couple had met again at Sandringham and later spent some time together after a polo match in Sussex.

A relationship with a member of the royal family could not remain private for long – and privacy would soon become a rare commodity for Diana.

The media were about to discover her; she would become their most popular and fascinating subject. And the public's appetite for information about her would grow to insatiable proportions.

The Fairy Tale Begins...

D iana's love/hate relationship with the camera lens began in September 1980, when a reporter and two eagle-eyed photographers spotted the Prince of Wales fishing on the banks of the River Dee.

growing news story. The flat in Coleherne Court was 'doorstepped' at all hours by photographers anxious to grab that all-important latest picture and reporters wanting the answer to *that* question.

Lady Diana was invariably polite and courteous to the members of the press pack.

Diana poses in the sunshine

Accompanying the Prince was a teenage girl attempting to hide behind a tree. She eventually emerged with a cap and a head scarf concealing her face and hurriedly disappeared over the brow of a hill.

From then on rumours of a royal romance spread like wildfire. The attractive kindergarten teacher – soon to be dubbed 'Shy Di' – became the focal point of a constantly

They pursued her for five months, during which she categorically refused to confirm the royal romance.

On one famous occasion she agreed to pose for the cameras out in the summer sunshine, along with two of the toddlers in her care. When the pictures appeared in the following day's press they showed 'Shy Di' in a flimsy dress, back-lit by the sun which revealed

The Fairy
Tale Begins…

Earl Spencer proudly leads his daughter into St Paul's Cathedral

Bride and groom emerge from St Paul's

her shapely legs. She was embarrassed and tearful at the exposure. But it was a lesson well-learned and one that would make her more wary of the press in future.

However, her embarrassment was quelled by Prince Charles' reaction to the picture. 'I knew your legs were good,' he said. 'But I didn't realise they were that spectacular.'

The incident also brought about a tightening of security. Charles and Diana were not seen together in public for another month. It was then that they attended a race meeting in Ludlow, Shropshire, during which the Prince rode in a race for amateur jockeys. They were both at the meeting, but were not seen *together*.

The couple met on several occasions during the following months. Then, in February 1981, shortly after Lady Diana's return from a

holiday with her mother in Australia and Prince Charles' return from a skiing vacation in Switzerland, Charles proposed marriage.

On 24 February 1981, Buckingham Palace issued a statement: 'It is with the greatest pleasure that the Queen and the Duke of Edinburgh announce the betrothal of their beloved son, The Prince of Wales, to the Lady Diana Spencer, daughter of the Earl Spencer and the Honourable Mrs Shand-Kydd.'

Diana vacated her flat almost immediately, imploring her flatmates: 'For God's sake ring me up, I'm going to need you.'

She moved into Clarence House, the London home of the Queen Mother, and prepared for the wedding which would take place on 29 July in St Paul's Cathedral.

After many months of speculation, of wondering and waiting, this was precisely the

tonic that the British nation needed. It was good news for a change, and crowds of well-wishers crowded outside Buckingham Palace.

At another famous photo-call, in the garden at Buckingham Palace, Diana proudly showed off her engagement ring – a wonderful sapphire surrounded by fourteen diamonds on a platinum base. Later, with her fiancé by her side, she gave her first media interview, shyly saying: 'It is always nice when there are two of you and there's someone there to help you.' Asked if she was in love, she replied: 'Of course.'

And the Prince added: 'Whatever love is.' It was an off-the-cuff remark that would later return to haunt the couple.

The Royal Wedding was *the* event of 1981. People came from all over the country and

The Royal Wedding was 'the' event of 1981

The Fairy Tale Begins...

from all parts of the world to witness history in the making. Vast crowds lined the route of the wedding procession, as the fabulous Glass Coach conveyed Diana and her father (who had only recently recovered from illness) from Buckingham Palace to the steps of St Paul's Cathedral.

There she stepped out of the coach to reveal for the first time her spectacular Emanuel wedding gown and its magnificent train. When the train had been properly arranged behind her, by Elizabeth Emanuel and the bridesmaids, Diana and her father made their way into the Cathedral where 2,500 guests, including numerous monarchs and heads of state, awaited the Wedding of the Century.

The stirring ceremony, conducted by the Archbishop of Canterbury, was seen all over the world by an estimated 750 million TV viewers. During the exchange of vows both Charles and Diana fluffed their responses, but out in the streets everyone cheered when they uttered the magic words: 'I will'.

The Archbishop remarked that the moment was '...the stuff of which fairy tales were made'.

The happy couple returned to Buckingham Palace in the open landau that had previously carried Prince Charles, and his best man Prince Andrew, to St Paul's. Tumultuous cheers greeted them every inch of the way.

Later they appeared four times on the palace balcony, together with the rest of the royal family. On their fourth appearance,

At Balmoral after the honeymoon

The Fairy Tale Begins...

that famous kiss seemed to make the fairy tale complete.

The honeymoon saw the newlyweds on a two-week cruise in the southern Mediterranean, aboard the Royal Yacht *Britannia*. They sailed a

course that somehow managed to avoid the news-hungry media. After their honeymoon the couple were welcomed back by the royal family at Balmoral.

Diana was a big hit with everyone

They settled in at Kensington Palace and often spent weekends at Highgrove House, in Gloucestershire.

Prince Charles was approaching his 33rd birthday and already well set in his ways. Diana was just a few weeks past her 20th birthday and her true personality had yet to emerge.

Diana's charisma quotient was evident on her very first official engagement with her husband – a three-day tour of Wales. Arriving in Caernarfon on a bitterly cold October day, she was dressed in the Welsh national colours, red and green, and sympathised with everyone who had waited so long to greet her.

On 5 November, Diana's pregnancy was announced by Buckingham Palace – news that was greeted with great joy everywhere. On a visit to York the royal couple were even showered with baby clothes and cuddly toys.

In the coming weeks it became necessary for her to cancel a number of public engagements, prompting great concern about her health.

December saw Diana's first solo engagement when she switched on Christmas lights in London's West End. As she pressed the button and the lights flickered to life, she was greeted with a tumultuous cheer.

In February 1982 the royal couple were holidaying in the Bahamas, when a photographer snapped some candid shots of the pregnant Princess wearing a bikini. These pictures duly appeared in the press and taught Diana another salutary lesson, about the sometimes over-intrusive nature of the media.

It rained throughout the rest of the tour, but nothing could dampen the enthusiasm of the Welsh people for their Princess, nor hers for them. She was a big hit with everyone, young and old.

On the third day the Prince and Princess visited a maternity hospital in the Rhondda Valley. Someone asked if she would soon be starting a family of her own. In response to the question, Diana simply smiled her now famous shy smile. In fact, she was already pregnant.

The tour ended with Diana making her first public speech, in which she spoke in Welsh of her pride at being 'Princess of such a wonderful place, and of the Welsh, who are very special to me'.

This, however, was just one symptom of the pressures of royal life which the Princess was beginning to feel so keenly. Behind the scenes she was already suffering private agonies that would eventually become public knowledge.

Motherhood

The proud parents leave hospital with Prince William

Prince William of Wales was born on the evening of 21 June 1982, in the Lindo Wing of St Mary's Hospital in Paddington. Prince Charles, who was present at the birth, said he was: 'Relieved... delighted... overwhelmed'.

Next day, looking frail but happy and accompanied by her husband, the young Princess left the hospital carrying her new son in her arms. Two weeks later the child was christened in the Music Room at Buckingham Palace.

In March 1983, the nine-month old Prince William became a jet-set baby when he was taken to Australia – at Diana's insistence – to join the royal couple who were on an official tour down-under.

It was on this visit that Diana's star truly rose. She triumphed wherever she went in Australia and New Zealand. The people loved her, and Prince Charles became almost a background figure. He even joked with the crowd saying: 'I wish I had two wives. I'll have to split Diana in half so she can walk on both sides of the street' ...and... 'You've got *me*, you'd better ask for your money back!'

It was the same story when the royal couple visited Canada a few months later. Once again Diana was the star of the show; Charles was the straight man. On this visit, however, Prince William was left at home and Diana missed him terribly.

In February 1984 it was announced that the Princess of Wales was expecting her second child. Seven months later, on 15 September, Prince Henry of Wales entered the world at St Mary's Hospital. It was later announced that he would be known as 'Prince Harry'.

This time, when the Prince and Princess of Wales emerged from the hospital with their new baby, Diana looked a picture of health and radiance.

The two Princes would grow up largely protected from the glare of the world-wide publicity machine that constantly dogged the footsteps of their mother.

Motherhood

Diana with the young Prince Harry

Diana joins in on sports day

Diana
International Icon

While carrying out her royal duties and engagements at home and abroad, Princess Diana quickly achieved a level of global fame and popularity that seemed to eclipse rock stars, movie stars, heads of state and even members of her new family.

Practically any story about her became headline news in the press and on radio and TV.

The camera loved her; she was photogenic. Her face appeared on countless magazine covers, more often than not increasing the circulation figures of those publications.

With her slim figure, long legs and glamorous looks, she became a Queen of Fashion. Her outfits were scrutinised in minute detail by the fashion writers. Young women everywhere were influenced by her sense of style: her dresses, hats, shoes and hairstyles were copied around the world. Diana was as important to the 'rag trade' as a whole army of supermodels.

While adhering to royal protocol on public engagements, the Princess did not particularly enjoy the same private pursuits as her husband. Polo and country pastimes, such as hunting, shooting and fishing, were tolerated, but they were not really for her. She did not even like riding and confessed to a fear of horses (which she later overcame).

A traditional Maori greeting in New Zealand

Any story about her became headline news

Diana was always popular in Australia

Diana
International Icon

Diana preferred the more artistic areas of ballet, opera, cinema and pop music. She also preferred the company of a younger circle of friends and did not get along particularly well with some of her husband's older, more intellectual, associates.

The fun-loving side of Diana's nature often bubbled to the surface, sometimes in the company of her good friend Sarah, Duchess of York, who had married Prince Andrew in 1986.

On those occasions when 'Fergie and Di' were caught on camera while clowning around, the resulting pictures invariably made the headlines and caused more than a few frowns within the establishment.

Diana's high profile was a great boon to those charities which she so wholeheartedly supported. And, as she matured, it was this aspect of her work that gradually became most important to her.

Among the many worthy causes to which Diana first leant her patronage were: The Welsh National Opera, the National Children's Orchestra, the Malcolm Sargent Cancer Fund for Children, the Royal School for the Blind and the Pre-School Playgroups Association.

On becoming patron of the British Deaf Association in 1983, Diana took lessons in sign language, which she would later use on

Diana in Egypt

Appointment at the Vatican

Dancing in Australia

The People's
Princess 21

Diana
International Icon

With Nancy Reagan

behalf of the Association. The following year saw her take on the presidency of Barnardos and the patronage of Birthright.

Later causes helped by the Princess included: The Royal Marsden Hospital, the National Hospital for Neurology and Neurosurgery, the Guinness Trust, Help the Aged, the British Red Cross, the National Meningitis Trust, Relate, Turning Point and the Great Ormond Street Hospital for Sick Children (where Prince William was once given emergency treatment following a serious accident at school).

She was always a sensation

In 1991, the year of her 30th birthday, Diana highlighted the plight of the homeless, and made her first attempts at demystifying the subject of Aids.

On a visit to the Middlesex Hospital, she said: 'HIV does not make people dangerous to know, so you can shake their hands and give them a hug – heaven knows they need it'.

With Luciano Pavarotti

To underline the sincerity of her words, she later held the hand of an Aids patient.

The Princess also supported the cause of leprosy and became patron of the Leprosy Mission in Britain.

Diana was always a sensation when she made an appearance on behalf of one of her causes. She took the time to talk to people, especially children, often going out of her way to ensure that no-one was neglected.

On several occasions Diana included her sons on her charity missions, in order to give them a broader understanding of the real world beyond the palace gates.

The amount of money Diana helped to raise for all of these good causes must surely be counted in many millions.

A skiing trip with the Duchess of York

The Fairy

Nineteen-ninety-two saw the publication of Andrew Morton's book *Diana: Her True Story*, written with the indirect approval of the Princess herself and based largely on interviews with her close friends. The book became a runaway best-seller as it purported to detail the breakdown of the marriage of the Prince and Princess of Wales.

The rift, it seemed, had begun very early in the marriage and simply grew to unbridgable proportions. There were revelations of rows and tantrums; of Diana's eating disorder, her depressions and of her 'suicide attempts'.

The book portrayed Prince Charles as the villain of the piece and told of his liaison with another woman, Camilla Parker Bowles.

Everyone knew that the relationship between Charles and Diana had been deteriorating for some time. On a royal tour in India with her husband, Diana was photographed sitting alone in front of the Taj Mahal – an image which simply emphasised the ever-widening gulf between the couple.

Things got worse in August 1992, when revelations were made regarding Diana's past relationship with James Gilbey, an Old Etonian, who was the subject of the so-called 'Squidgygate' tapes.

There was a royal tour of Korea, during which the strained relationship between Charles and Diana was plainly evident.

Shortly afterwards, in December 1992,

the then-Prime Minister, John Major, announced in the House of Commons that the Prince and Princess of Wales were to separate. It was, he explained, a joint decision.

In future Prince Charles would reside chiefly at Highgrove House, while Princess Diana would stay on at Kensington Palace.

Tale Ends

The attention of the media did not subside for the Princess; if anything it grew in intensity.

In November 1993, secretly taken photographs of Diana working-out in a London gym appeared in the press.

Then, in the summer of 1994, Prince Charles gave a television interview to his biographer Jonathan Dimbleby. The most sensational part of the programme was the Prince's admission that when his marriage 'became irretrievably broken down' he had been unfaithful to his wife.

He also said that: 'Those who marry into my family find it increasingly difficult to do so because of the added pressure. The stresses and strains become almost intolerable'.

Thirteen months after the separation, Diana announced to the world that she intended to reduce her official engagements in order to spend more time on her private life.

In an emotional speech, she said: 'I hope you can find it in your heart to understand and to give me the time and space so lacking in recent years... Your kindness and affection have carried me through some of the most difficult periods, and always your love and care have eased that journey'.

One consequence of this leap for freedom was Diana's decision to relinquish the security afforded by the official bodyguards who had been part of her life for over twelve years.

At the time there were no plans for a divorce.

In her Christmas speech, the Queen dubbed 1992 her *'annus horribilis'*.

Early in 1993 the royal saga took another twist with the revelation of an intimate taped telephone conversation, between Prince Charles and Camilla Parker Bowles.

The stories did not go away. There was another book, *Princess in Love*, which told of her close friendship with Major James Hewitt.

The Fairy Tale Ends

In November 1995 Diana appeared in the sensational *Panorama* interview, and with amazing frankness talked to Martin Bashir of her life inside the royal family.

She spoke about her relationship with James Hewitt, saying: 'I adored him ... but he let me down'.

Of her marriage she said: 'I desperately loved my husband and I wanted to share everything together and I thought we were a very good team'. But she also added: 'There were three of us in this marriage, so it was a bit crowded'.

"I'd like to be a Queen of People's Hearts."

Of her own hopes for the future Diana said: 'I'd like to be an ambassador ... to represent this country abroad... I'm not a political animal but I think the biggest disease the world suffers from today is the disease of people feeling unloved and I know that I can give love for a minute, for a day, for a month, but I can give – I'm happy to do that... I think the British people need someone in public life to give affection. I lead from the heart not the head... I'd like to be a queen of people's hearts, but I don't see myself as queen of this country'.

Within a month of the interview, Queen Elizabeth had urged her eldest son and her daughter-in-law to divorce.

The divorce was made absolute on 28 August 1996. Diana received a settlement estimated at some £17 million, but she lost her 'HRH' prefix, and would now be titled 'Diana, Princess of Wales'.

The 'fairy tale' was over.

Alone at the Taj Mahal

A New Life

In redefining her life Diana decided to resign her patronage of many charities in order to concentrate on the half dozen closest to her heart. They were: The National Aids Trust, The English National Ballet, The Royal Marsden NHS Trust, The Leprosy Mission, Great Ormond Street Hospital for Sick Children and Centrepoint.

Through the British Red Cross the Princess also became involved with her last months of her life – especially her friendship with Dodi Al Fayed.

Dodi was the 41-year-old son of Mohamed Al Fayed, the Egyptian-born, multi-millionaire owner of Harrods and a number of other top-notch establishments.

Dodi had been educated in Switzerland and had attended an officer training course at Sandhurst during his national service.

After his military service, he settled in London – and enjoyed the high life for a while. He gained a reputation as a jet-setting playboy

Diana with Jemima Khan

With Henry Kissinger in New York

great campaign – to rid the world of landmines. To this end she visited many victims of this dreadful legacy of the recent conflicts in Angola and Bosnia.

In the week before she died, the Princess gave what proved to be her last ever interview, in the French newspaper *Le Monde*, in which she spoke of the landmines issue.

But it was Diana's private life that dominated the headlines during the last two and was often seen in the company of beautiful women. He was married briefly to the model Suzanne Gregard; they divorced in 1987.

He was also a Hollywood film producer. Among the hit movies he was associated with were the Oscar-winning *Chariots of Fire* and Steven Spielberg's *Hook*.

Dodi had first met Diana several years earlier, when he mixed in Prince Charles' polo-playing circle. Their paths crossed on several

At the premiere of Richard Attenborough's *In Love and War*

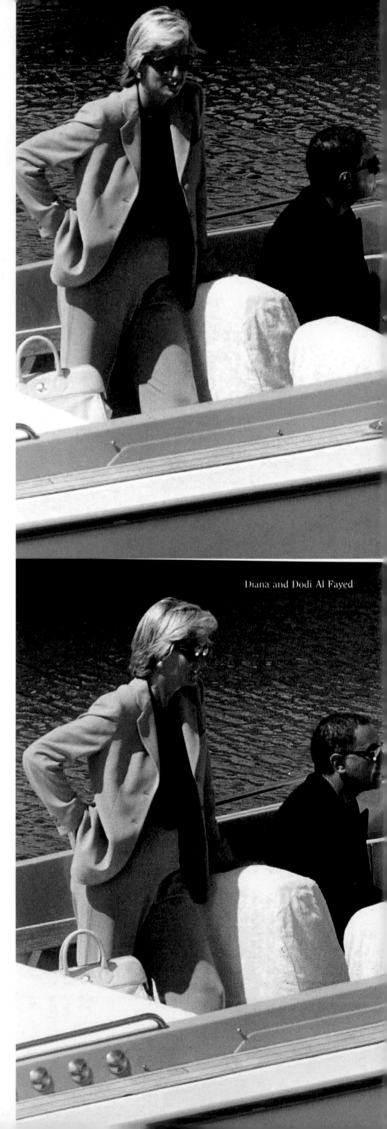

A New *Life*

occasions after that, but it was only in the summer of 1997 that they became close.

In early July Diana, Dodi and the Princes William and Harry spent ten days at the Al Fayed mansion in St Tropez. The boys, it was said, got along well with the outgoing Dodi.

At the end of July, Diana again joined Dodi, for a six-day cruise in the Mediterranean on board the Fayed's luxury yacht *Jonikal*.

Back in London, on 7 August, the couple enjoyed dinner at Dodi's apartment in Park Lane. Next day Diana flew to Bosnia on behalf of the landmines campaign.

The Princess seemed to be quite open about the relationship

On 21 August the *Jonikal* set sail from St Tropez, with Diana and Dodi on board. Three days later they dropped anchor in Portofino, Italy. Then it was on to the island of Sardinia where they stayed until flying back to Le Bourget airport, on the northern outskirts of Paris, on Saturday 30 August.

Throughout these summer jaunts, Dodi and Diana had grown closer. The Princess did not attempt to hide the fact and appeared to be quite open about the relationship. Sources close to Dodi said he was besotted with Diana – and she with him.

Several times they had been snapped by the long lenses of the photographers who were attempting to monitor their every move. Pictures of the couple holidaying together had appeared in newspapers all over the world.

As they made their way towards Paris on Saturday afternoon, the cameras were there again.

Diana and Dodi Al Fayed

On Sunday 31 August 1997, Great Britain awoke to the shocking news that both Diana and Dodi had died in Paris. That plain, simple statement gave rise to what must be the biggest outpouring of public grieving the country has ever seen.

And things only got worse as details of the tragedy unfolded.

On the Saturday evening Diana and Dodi had enjoyed a romantic dinner at the Ritz Hotel, an establishment owned by Dodi's father,

The biggest outpouring of public grieving the country has ever seen

in the Place Vendome. It was later reported that during the evening, Dodi had presented Diana with a ring.

Next day, they were to part for a while, and Diana was due to return to England and a reunion with her sons.

A number of 'paparazzi' were waiting outside the front of the hotel. These lensmen have long been a regular part of the celebrity scene in Paris. They were eager to grab the latest pictures of Diana and Dodi.

It didn't matter that the couple were doing something as innocuous as leaving a hotel; the point was that these would be the *latest* pictures.

Tragically, as it turned out, the results of this pursuit would also provide the last pictures of the couple.

Shortly after midnight, at the rear of the Ritz, Diana and Dodi, along with Dodi's

The Saddest Week Of The Year

British-born bodyguard, Trevor Rees-Jones, got into a powerful Mercedes S-Class limousine, driven by a stand-in chauffeur. Dodi's regular driver was being used as a decoy – a tactic which had apparently shaken-off photographers in London in the past.

Unfortunately, the ruse did not succeed on this occasion.

As the car sped away, the photographers followed on motorcycles. The fateful crash, in an underpass beneath the Place De L'Alma, was only minutes away.

The driver and Dodi were killed instantly. Trevor Rees-Jones survived the accident, but would then spend a long period in hospital.

The Princess of Wales was trapped inside the wreckage. She was eventually taken to the Pitie Salpetriere Hospital where, despite strenuous efforts to revive her, sadly, she passed away.

An official investigation began almost immediately, and this will no doubt eventually unearth the truth of the matter.

Whatever the root cause of the tragedy, we are left with one immutable fact: The

A river of emotion

Princess of Wales and her friend Dodi Al Fayed are with us no more. Prince Charles, together with Diana's sisters Lady Sarah and Lady Jane, flew to Paris on Sunday afternoon, to escort the Princess's body back to Britain.

Draped in the royal standard, Diana's coffin arrived in the early evening at RAF Northolt. Waiting there was the Prime Minister and the Defence Secretary. And many people left flowers inside the gates of the airfield.

To comply with Muslim tradition, Dodi Al Fayed was buried within twenty-four hours of his death. Following a funeral prayer at London's Central Mosque, his remains were interred at Brookwood Cemetery, near Woking in Surrey.

Diana's funeral took place on Saturday 6 September.

The days leading up to the sad event witnessed an incredible and intense outpouring of public grief and mourning. What began as a steady trickle of people leaving flowers outside Kensington, St James's and Buckingham Palaces, grew to an absolute river of emotion.

As it became more and more apparent

Diana's coffin arrives in England

just how large the crowds would be on the Saturday, the route of the funeral procession was extended, and would now begin at Kensington Palace, rather than St James's.

The route that would carry Diana's coffin out of London towards her final resting place in Althorp, was published – so that mourners throughout north London could pay their last respects.

As Diana's body lay at rest inside St. James's Palace, people queued for hours on end – many waited patiently overnight – in order to sign one of the special Books of Condolence inside the Palace. Similar books were signed all over the British Isles.

Sporting events due to take place on the day of the funeral were postponed as a mark of respect. These included Scotland's World Cup qualifying match with Belarus, but only after a public outcry. Three players in the squad had said they would not play if the match went ahead on the Saturday.

Supermarkets, shops, building societies and other firms closed down or altered their hours of business so that everyone could pay their last respects.

Even politics were put on hold. In Scotland and Wales the devolution campaigns were suspended during the mourning period.

Shock waves of grief were felt all over the world.

Many Britons were abroad on holiday; some returned early to pay their respects.

Throughout the Commonwealth Territories the flags flew at half-mast and Books of Condolence were signed. The people of the troubled island of Monserrat called for their new capital to be named 'Port Diana'.

In Japan hundreds of bouquets were left at the British Embassy in Tokyo, and thousands

The Saddest Week Of The Year

queued there to sign the Book of Condolence.

In the USA, where they regarded Diana as one of their own, the news was greeted with utter disbelief. At the MTV Awards in New York, Madonna said: 'It is time for us to take responsibility for our own insatiable need to run after gossip and scandal and lies and rumour... we are all one, and until we change our negative behaviour, tragedies like this will continue to occur'.

At the same function, the Spice Girls dedicated their Best Dance Video award to Diana. Mel C said: 'Princess Diana is a great loss to our country. She was a fantastic ambassador for Great Britain'.

Geri added: 'I think what we are really about is what Lady Diana had, real Girl Power'.

The Royal Family stayed at Balmoral until Thursday. This was interpreted by many to mean that they were insensitive to the feelings of the nation.

It may be that the royals misjudged the mood of the people, and perhaps an earlier return to the capital would have been advisable.

Whatever the rights and wrongs of the situation, they were sharing a family's private grief. They were consoling Prince William and Prince Harry and preparing the boys for the ordeal that still lay ahead.

Prince Charles and his sons arrived in London on Friday afternoon when they looked at the floral tributes and met members of the public outside Kensington Palace. At about the same time, the Queen and Prince Philip were walking in the Mall and speaking to mourners there.

At six o'clock that evening the Queen made an unprecedented live speech to the nation in which she described Diana as 'an exceptional and gifted person. In good times and bad, she never lost her capacity to smile or laugh, nor to inspire others with her warmth and kindness'.

Her Majesty also said: 'I for one believe that there are lessons to be drawn from her life, and from the extraordinary and moving reaction to her death'.

"In good times and bad, she never lost her capacity to smile or laugh."

The speech and the earlier 'walkabouts' by the royals went some way towards calming the previous unsettled mood of the majority of the nation.

The sun was setting on Friday evening, when Diana's coffin was transported from St James's Palace to spend the night in Kensington Palace, the magnificent building in which she had once lived. Every inch of the route was lined with crowds, up to twenty deep in places. They watched the hearse, followed by a limousine carrying Charles and the young Princes. It was an almost eerie sight as countless flashlights illuminated the interiors of the two vehicles.

Almost unbelievably on that sad evening came news of the death of Diana's soulmate, Mother Teresa of Calcutta. The world-renowned humanitarian had been awarded the Nobel Peace Prize in 1979, for her work among the poor and destitute. She and Diana – two women united by a common goal – had met eight times since 1992 and had become firm friends.

The Queen addresses the nation

Queuing to sign the Books of Condolence at St James's Palace

Goodbye England's Rose

It was estimated that over a million people lined the route of Diana's funeral procession on Saturday 6 September.

Many others decided to watch the event unfold on the giant TV screens set-up in three London parks. Elsewhere across the world, some 2 1/2 billion people saw televised pictures of the funeral.

The sun shone for Diana. It was a perfect, cloudless, English summer's morning as the

guardsmen from the Prince of Wales' Company, 1st Battalion, Welsh Guards. These were the pall bearers who would have the task of carrying the coffin into the Abbey.

Laying atop the coffin were three wreaths from Prince William, Prince Harry and Diana's brother, the Earl Spencer. Poignantly, Harry's wreath bore a card in an envelope on which he had written the word 'Mummy'.

As the cortege moved slowly along the route, each passing minute was marked by the tolling of a single bell at Westminster Abbey.

The funeral cortege passes the Royal Family at Buckingham Palace

cortege set out from Kensington Palace at 9:08.

Draped in a royal standard edged with ceremonial ermine, the coffin was borne on a gun carriage drawn by members of the King's Troop Horse Artillery. It was accompanied by

At practically every step of the way flowers were thrown in the direction of the flag-draped coffin. There was little sound beyond the quiet rustle of the crowd, of weeping, of the clip-clop of hooves on the streets and of the

Goodbye England's
Rose

occasional whinny from the horses.

At 9:24 the cortege turned into Hyde Park at the Queen's Gate entrance. By 10:02 it had reached Hyde Park Corner, where it passed through the Wellington Arch.

At 10:20 Diana's coffin passed Buckingham Palace, where stood the Queen, the Queen Mother and other members of the extended Royal Family, who bowed their heads as the cortege passed by.

Five minutes after passing Buckingham Palace, the cortege reached St James's Palace, where Diana's body had lain throughout most of the week.

There, showing commendable courage beyond their years, the two young Princes joined their mother for the final mile to the Abbey. Together with

Tom Hanks, Tom Cruise and Nicole Kidman arrive at Westminster Abbey

their father, their grandfather Prince Philip, and their uncle the Earl Spencer, they stepped behind the gun carriage.

Also joining the procession at this point were the 533 specially invited guests, representing the numerous charities that had been so close to Diana's heart.

At 10:39 the crunch of boots on gravel was heard as the cortege began to cross Horseguards Parade. Two minutes later it turned right, into Whitehall, to pass the offices of state, the entrance to Downing Street (home of the Prime Minister) and the Cenotaph.

It was then, as the Queen left for the Abbey, that the royal standard atop Buckingham Palace was replaced by the Union Flag flying at half-mast. This break with protocol brought another rush of emotion and loud applause from those outside the Palace and those watching the big screens in the parks.

Into Parliament Square moved the cortege, past Big Ben and the Houses of Parliament, before turning right, towards Broad Sanctuary and Westminster Abbey itself.

By now all the invited guests had taken their places inside the Abbey. The guest list was drawn from all walks of Diana's life. Beside the many members of the royal family, were Diana's mother Frances Shand-Kydd, her sisters, her brother and her step-mother Raine (now Comtesse de Chambrun).

Many of Diana's friends were among the congregation, as were several of her household staff. The political figures present included the Prime Minister and four of his predecessors. From abroad came Hilary Clinton and Bernadette Chirac.

From the world of cinema came Tom Cruise, Nicole Kidman, Tom Hanks, Steven Spielberg and Lord Richard Attenborough. Among those representing the recording industry were Elton John, George Michael, Sting, Shirley Bassey, Diana Ross, Sir Cliff Richard, Chris De Burgh, Bryan Adams – and

Princes William and Harry wait to join the cortege

the great opera singer Luciano Pavarotti.

The small screen was represented by Michael Barrymore, Clive James, Sir David Frost and Ruby Wax.

Fashion gurus Valentino, Bruce Oldfield, Karl Lagerfeld and the Emanuels were there. So, too, was Donatella Versace, whose brother's funeral Diana had attended only weeks before.

At 10:43, the Queen, the Queen Mother and Prince Edward were received at the Great West Door of the Abbey, by the Very Reverend Dr Wesley Carr, the Dean of Westminster.

Shortly afterwards the specially selected Welsh Guardsmen who had marched beside the gun carriage for the last four miles, removed their bearskin hats and carefully lifted the coffin onto their shoulders. After the National Anthem, they slowly carried it into the Quire and Sacrarium.

The service began precisely at 11:00 and was relayed via speakers to all those standing outside the Abbey and in Whitehall.

It was a very moving service, in which Diana's sisters both gave a reading, before Prime Minister Tony Blair read the famous 'Through A Glass, Darkly' passage from 1 Corinthians 13.

Then Elton John sang 'Candle In The Wind'. Originally written as an homage to Marylin Monroe, the song's lyrics had been rewritten as a tribute to Diana. They began: 'Goodbye England's rose, may you ever grow in our hearts...' And went on: 'Now you belong to heaven, and the stars spell out your name'.

Throats tightened and tears flowed as the words and music were beamed across the capital, throughout Britain and around the world.

Next came the Tribute from Diana's brother, the 9th Earl Spencer. His was a stinging

Goodbye England's *Rose*

The Princes join the procession

speech, of which every word found it's target.

The Earl spoke of: 'A country in mourning, a world in shock' at the death of his sister, whom he described as 'the very essence of compassion, of duty, of style and beauty. All over the world she was a symbol of selfless humanity'.

He said: 'She needed no royal title to generate her particular brand of magic'.

Of her charity work: 'Without your God-given sensitivity we would be immersed in greater ignorance of the anguish of Aids and HIV sufferers, the plight of the homeless, the isolation of lepers, the random destruction of landmines... Diana explained to me once that it was her innermost feelings of suffering that made it possible for her to connect with her constituency of the rejected'.

He touched upon his sister's vulnerability: '...for all the status, the glamour, the applause, Diana remained throughout a very insecure person at heart, almost childlike in her desire to do good for others...'

The Earl spoke of Diana's visit to his home in South Africa in March, and the fact that they had managed to shield her from 'the ever-present paparazzi'.

He talked of their childhood together and paid tribute to: 'her level-headedness and strength' and the fact that 'despite the most bizarre-like life imaginable after her childhood she remained... true to herself'.

He said that Diana often talked of leaving England: '...mainly because of the treatment she received at the hands of the newspapers'.

The Earl then said that Princes William and Harry should be protected from a similar fate, and pledged to Diana that his family would do all it could 'to continue the imaginative and loving way in which you were steering these

Elton John arrives at the Abbey

The Princes and Earl Spencer watch in sadness

Diana's coffin leaves the Abbey

Approaching Westminster Abbey

Below: The Dean of Westminster greets the Queen

two exceptional young men so that their souls are not simply immersed by duty and tradition but can sing openly as you planned'.

He closed by saying: 'Above all we give thanks for the life of a woman I am so proud to be able to call my sister. The unique, the complex, the extraordinary and irreplaceable Diana whose beauty, both internal and external, will never be extinguished from our minds'.

As the Earl returned silently to his seat, spontaneous applause was heard from those who had listened via the speakers outside the Abbey. Then, as Lord Richard Attenborough later noted: 'It came inside like a forest fire'.

And suddenly the whole of the Abbey was filled with applause – something that had never happened at a funeral of this magnitude before. Another guest, Chris De Burgh, later said it was 'Awesome'.

The service concluded with a minute's silence – a silence that reverberated around the world, as people everywhere reflected in peace.

When the service was over, Diana's coffin was driven in a hearse along part of the route which the cortege had taken earlier. Then, at Hyde Park Corner, it turned into Park Lane and headed towards north London.

All along the route, people lined the streets to say goodbye to their Princess. By the time the hearse reached the M1 motorway, its windscreen was half-covered in flowers that had to be cleared away.

All along the motorway, on bridges and embankments, and on the southbound carriageway where the traffic had stopped, people waited anxiously for Diana to pass by.

At Junction 15A, in Northamptonshire, the hearse left the M1 to wend its way towards Diana's final resting place.

Earlier in the week the Spencer family had decided that she should be buried on a small wooded island in the Oval Lake at Althorp House, rather than in the local parish churchyard. In this way they could look after Diana's grave and afford privacy to her sons when they visit in the future. (For a few weeks each year the site will be open to the public.)

People lined the country roads and by mid-afternoon, when the cortege arrived at the gates of Althorp House, the hearse was again covered with flowers.

When it drove into the beautiful grounds, two policemen closed the heavy iron gates. Shortly afterwards Diana, Princess of Wales, was buried in a quiet, private ceremony.

Goodbye England's *Rose*

Unlike many of the 'great and good', Diana demonstrated by her actions that she was *both*. That is why so many, many people mourned her passing.

She was, as Tony Blair said on the morning of her death, 'the People's Princess'.

Had she lived on she might have become a 'goodwill ambassador' for Britain. It was

She achieved so much in her lifetime.

reported that the Prime Minister had recently discussed the possibilty of such a role with her.

She achieved so much in her lifetime. Perhaps, with better understanding and guidance, she would have achieved so much more.

In different circumstances – and if the 'fairy tale' had come true – she might one day have become the Queen of England.

As things turned out in her short, turbulent and ultimately tragic story, Diana, Princess of Wales, ended her life as the Queen of People's Hearts.

Beside all the fond memories imprinted on the hearts and minds of people everywhere, perhaps two of her finest legacies will be the private influence she exerted on her sons William and Harry; and the living, working memorial that is The Diana, Princess of Wales Memorial Fund.

Donations flooding into the Fund will add to the many millions of pounds raised in her lifetime for those charities that were closest to her heart.

Diana, Princess of Wales, will never be forgotten.

Dodi's father, Mohamed Al Fayed, after the funeral

Hilary Clinton represented the USA

The hearse carries Diana home to Althorp